MW01295078

BEFORE ONBOARDING

*How to Integrate New Leaders for Quick
and Sustained Results*

Michael K. Burroughs

To Jan.
My wife,
My partner,
My best friend,
and the love of my life.

CONTENTS

ACKNOWLEDGEMENTS

Anyone who has ever attempted to write a book of any kind knows what a daunting task it is. Underestimating the work involved is common, as is anticipating how many people are ultimately involved in the finished product. This book is no exception. I am indebted to many for their inspiration and their direct assistance.

Dr. Dan Patterson was a client when we met. An HR and OD professional and like me, a retired military officer, Dan graciously agreed to review this book and advise me on how to improve it. Another HR executive, Sue Wilkerson, first encouraged (and retained) me to combine the New Leader Integration process outlined in this book with an executive recruiting project, and a new, innovative service was born. She too was a reviewer of my manuscript. Robin Singleton, Global Practice Leader for Healthcare at DHR

International, has believed in and championed New Leader Integration from the moment she first heard about it. James Abruzzo, Global Practice Leader for Nonprofits, also encouraged me to incorporate the process into our executive recruiting projects. Joe Christman, Global Sector Leader for Aerospace and Defense, has also been a strong supporter of New Leader Integration and encouraged me in making the process available to DHR's executive search clients. David Hoffmann, Chairman and CEO of DHR International, committed the firm's resources to building a consulting business line around the process. Sally Powers served as my boss for six years when I was VP of Organization Development in my last corporate position prior to entering the executive recruiting field. It was under her leadership that I fully developed, implemented and refined the New Leader Integration process detailed in this book. She championed my ideas throughout a multi-divisional company as I put the concept into practice. There would be no New Leader Integration process were it not for her support when it mattered most.

It takes many people to bring a book from an idea to a finished product. The fine people at CreateSpace were there with me throughout the process with timely presentation advice and design assistance.

Bringing a book into fruition for the first time requires stepping out into the unknown. Having people who believe in you is paramount. My parents, Tippie and Nancy Burroughs, have always assumed that whatever I set out to do I would accomplish. I have had 100% of their support in every professional step I have ever taken.

My two sons, Michael Jr. and John Burroughs, are amazing men. I have shared with many people through the years what a great blessing it is to have substantive and stimulating conversations with my adult sons and to learn from them. They are each outstanding leaders in their own right. They challenge me to think. Both have been a source of encouragement and guidance as I have embarked upon this project.

My wife, Janice Burroughs, is my rock. I have learned in life that it is best to heed her advice and counsel. I've done so here as well. Jan has lived the New Leader Integration concept with me from the very beginning—in the Army, where I first experienced a rudimentary leader integration process, to the present day—and has encouraged me to develop it, refine it and write about it. I dedicate this book to her.

PART I

THE NEW LEADER INTEGRATION LANDSCAPE

INTRODUCTION

Executive attrition statistics are alarming. They appear in multiple sources and are consistent. One source, the 2011 "Executive Transitions" study, was conducted jointly by The Institute of Executive Development and Alexcel Group. There were 150 participants in 18 different industries located in 22 countries who participated. The study concluded that:

- Ramp up time for new external hires is most commonly between six and nine months (36% agreed; 30% said over nine months).

- Ramp up time for internal transfers within the same organization was less but not by much (41% said three to six months; 34% said greater than six months).

- Thirty percent of executives who join an organization as an external hire fail within two years (27% are actually gone within two years).

- Twenty-three percent of executives who make internal transfers fail to meet expectations within two years.

The executive director of the Institute of Executive Development, Scott Saslow, is quoted as saying, "Typically, organizations work extremely hard to identify and hire new talent…but then rely on hope when it comes to making their new investment successful."

Michael Watkins of the Harvard Business School, in his seminal guide for leader integration, *The First 90 Days*, had interviewed 210 company CEOs and presidents as part of his research and concluded that:

- Each year over a half million managers enter new positions in the Fortune 500 alone.

- The failure rate for new leaders who enter organizations from outside is high. Studies have found that…40% to 50% of senior outside hires fail to achieve desired results.

- The actions new leaders take in the first three months in a new job will largely determine whether they ultimately succeed or fail.

- The Breakeven Point—the point at which a new leader has contributed more value than has been consumed from the organization—is 6.2 months.

He goes on to say that, "Given the stakes, it is surprising how little good guidance is available to new leaders about how to transition more effectively and efficiently into new roles." He concludes, "Adoption of a standard framework for accelerating executive transitions can yield big returns for organizations."[1]

This book, *Before Onboarding: How to Integrate New Leaders for Quick and Sustained Results*, details one such framework organizations can use to accelerate executive transitions. It is adaptable to most organizations. The objectives of this New Leader Integration process are:

- Compress leader integration time (to get the right results sooner).

- Avoid costly and potentially career ending mistakes.

- Minimize staff productivity declines and turnover related to leadership changes.

- Accelerate team cohesiveness with new leaders and their direct reports.

- Sustain the new leader's early successes over the long-term.

While onboarding programs are becoming more prolific in organizations today, they vary in scope and effectiveness. These programs are generally helpful processes with an

---

[1]   From "The First 90 Days: Critical Success Strategies for New Leaders at All Levels" by Michael D. Watkins. Harvard Business Press, 2003.

emphasis on administration, orientation, and role and responsibility clarification. Every organization should have a well designed onboarding program. The critical mass of onboarding efforts occurs after the new leader is, well…onboard.

While complementary, there is an important distinction between onboarding and the New Leader Integration process outlined in this book. New Leader Integration or "pre-boarding" occurs for the most part BEFORE the start date—not after. A consultant adept at change management oversees the effort. Think of New Leader Integration as a process that typically begins the day an offer is accepted, reaches a high point by the end of the new leader's first day on the job, and culminates 90 days later after a series of follow-up meetings at 30-day intervals with the process consultant, new leader and boss.

In the following pages I provide a template for a pre-boarding process and how to implement an effective New Leader Integration program. It is a guide, not an edict. It is intended that this book will encourage top executives to make the commitment to develop a comprehensive New Leader Integration program that works best for them. The process can easily be tailored to fit most organizations and the preferences of consultants, both internal and external, who would be called upon to implement the program. This book can be viewed as a step-by-step template to be implemented as it appears here or a springboard for creating your own new leader integration process. Any modifications, however, should include these features at a minimum:

- The process begins before the new leader's start date.

- It is overseen by a process consultant.

- It involves the new leader's boss, peers and direct reports (at a minimum) and

- It extends beyond the start date for at least the first 90 days.

CHAPTER 1

Why is New Leader Integration Needed?

A failed executive is a costly problem. These costs accumulate over time and include:

- Search fees (if an executive recruiter was involved)

- Relocation expenses

- Signing bonus

- Other bonuses

- Stock grants and options

- Downtime

- Decreased productivity of the work group

- Unanticipated turnover of valuable employees

These costs are more often than not chalked up to a "bad hire." It's easy to lay the blame at the feet of the failed executive. Let's assume for the moment that the hired executive had all the right stuff: education, experience, track record, aptitude, temperament, etc. Most organizations are initially satisfied with the new executive they have hired and are optimistic that their decision was the right one. This book is not intended to help you become better selectors of talent. Much has been written about that already.

When a new leader fails to meet expectations we should ask ourselves this question instead: What difference would it have made had we managed the integration of this executive rather than leave his or her success to chance? This book addresses that question head on. It is about improving the likelihood that the new leaders you hire or promote will succeed both in the short and long-term.

When I conduct an executive search, a frequent question asked of me is: "How long will this take?" More often than not by the time a search firm is engaged to recruit a new executive, the position has been a recognized need for a long time. When the search concludes (average time is 90 to 120 days), the hiring organization is already behind the power curve. Consider a scenario where the search was engaged to replace a floundering executive. In many cases, the decision to replace that individual took months—months added to those that will be needed to conduct a thorough replacement search. By the time the new executive arrives, the management team expects to see results quickly in order to make up for lost time. The attitude of most high-performing candidates is that, once hired, they must rapidly put their unique stamp on the new organization. They intend to hit the ground running and achieve some early wins. That's to be expected.

As we saw earlier, Michael Watkins of the Harvard Business School suggests that the ultimate success or failure of a new leader will often be determined in the first 90 days. It is the most critical time for all new leaders. Every day must count. It stands to reason that the downtime between an offer's acceptance and the start date is a perfect time to lay the groundwork for new leaders to achieve early successes. Once they have arrived, the opportunity will have passed.

When I have had this discussion with my search clients, some ask, "Who has time to wait 90 days?" This question further illustrates the high expectations organizations have to see quick results from a new leader they have hired or promoted in addition to the pressure that new leaders place on themselves to make a positive impact in a hurry. A method for addressing both is the aim of this book. What can be done "before day 1" to provide your future leaders every advantage in order to achieve a rapid and successful integration?

The New Leader Integration process detailed in the following pages will provide your organization significant benefits if it is given the attention it deserves, the right change agent facilitates the process, and the model is fully supported from the top and throughout the organization.

In this book I lay out a transitional framework for integrating new leaders into your organization and improving the likelihood that they will achieve the right results quickly, avoid costly and potentially career ending mistakes, and sustain their early wins over the long term.

CHAPTER 2

The New Leader Integration Model

There are six stages of this New Leader Integration process. They are:

- Entry

- Interviews

- Documentation

- Debriefing

- Kick-off Meeting

- Follow-up

Entry

It is important that all candidates in consideration for a new leadership position be informed that they will participate in a New Leader Integration process if hired. It will begin the day an offer is accepted. If the process consultant has been identified at that point, the candidates should be given the consultant's name and some background information. They can then do some research (e.g., LinkedIn, personal website, blog, etc.) to gain familiarity with the individual who would oversee the integration process.

New hires are likely engaged in exiting their current positions and possibly making plans to relocate family members. It is a very hectic time, but savvy new hires will already be mentally preparing for the change in jobs. Most executives have grown accustomed to navigating these waters solo. But the fact there is a New Leader Integration process designed to help them effectively transition into their new role should be well-received once the details are explained. This integration approach will be even better received when you are able to say that all new leaders in your organization participate in this process.

It is important to distinguish New Leader Integration from traditional onboarding. If the organization has an onboarding program, the new leader will be expected to participate in that as well. Onboarding, of course, starts for the most part when the new executive arrives for work. The more that can be accomplished in advance of the start date, the sooner the new leader will be up and running.

Let's assume at this point that an offer is in process or has already been accepted. The first step the organization will take is to reconnect the consultant with the new leader. This can be accomplished by phone or in person. Ideally, the consultant would have already met the candidates during the interview process (more on that later). It is important that the new leader develop a comfort level with the consultant as soon as possible. The consultant then reviews the integration plan (i.e., the people involved and questions to be asked) with the new leader and provides the opportunity to introduce questions he or she would like to have answered during those interviews.

After the introduction the consultant begins the second stage.

Interviews

The next step is to notify all participants involved in the New Leader Integration process to inform them they will be interviewed by an executive integration consultant prior to the start date of the new leader. They need to be briefed, if they do not know already, that the process is designed to focus the new leader during the transition by ensuring that he or she has the benefit of as much meaningful information and guidance as possible prior to the start date. The consultant will provide additional information to each individual in the process when they meet and will let them know that the only persons who will be privy to their individual comments will be the new leader and consultant.

At a minimum there are three segments of people to be interviewed. They are:

- Boss (or key members of the board of directors/ trustees)

- Peers (if there are any)

- Direct reports

The process is not limited to these three segments. Depending on the situation, there may also be others whose input would benefit the new leader (and themselves) such as:

- Key customers

- Major suppliers

- Physician group leaders

- Trustees

- Major donors

- Others

The Boss (or Members of the Board of Directors/Trustees) Interview

Let's assume for illustration purposes that the new leader reports to a president. The consultant would meet with the "boss" to obtain information, most of which would not likely have surfaced during the hiring process. This includes general information and specific guidance, along with the key success indicators the boss will use to evaluate the performance of the new leader, especially during the first 90 days. This information is so specific that it is broken down into 30- day increments for the first three months (more if it is important to do so, but the first 90 days is essential).

In the course of gathering this information, the consultant will also want to know what the new leader should NOT do, as well as what potential "land mines" may exist that need to be avoided. It is surprising to many bosses who participate in this process just how much meaningful guidance they are able to provide, IF ASKED, and how valuable that information, once compiled, will be to the new leader.

It is natural for bosses to be concerned about the ultimate success or failure of executives hired from outside the organization, but the same concerns are there when the new leader is being promoted from within or is coming across the organization as well, e.g., from one division to another. A good consultant will obtain a treasure trove of guidance during this meeting, whether it is for an outside hire or an internal appointment or promotion. Otherwise, it would take any new leader weeks or months to discover this information, and by then it could be too late to make a difference, or serious mistakes could have already been made.

If the new leader reports to a board of directors or trustees, the consultant would conduct these interviews with the persons most capable of providing the necessary guidance. More often than not, there are several people who will need to be interviewed. If there is conflicting information coming from those discussions, the consultant must gain clarification before moving forward. If there is no agreement (rare, but it happens), the consultant needs to note this as a potential problem for the incoming leader.

Board interviews will usually take longer to accomplish. They can be difficult to schedule. This is a potential obstacle, and someone within the organization should be assigned to arrange these meetings with board members. It is better to have them all in one location, scheduled apart, if possible, so the consultant can gather the necessary information efficiently. More than likely, though, an organization's board members will be disbursed. In these situations it may be necessary to do some of these interviews by phone, Skype or other videoconferencing means if travel is impractical.

Peer Interviews

The next segment to interview includes ALL of the new leader's peers. For example, if the new leader reports to a president, some likely peers would be the CFO, VP of HR, VP of Supply Chain, VP of Marketing, VP of Sales, and others. Most leaders have peers, but this is usually not the case with the top executive. In some situations, however, a top executive's peers may be people with whom he or she regularly interacts at a higher headquarters. The new leader's success is impacted by the ability to influence other executives outside of his or her line of authority. Peers will have opinions as to what the new leader should be doing (or avoiding). Peers will also, in most cases, have experience working with the new leader's predecessor, and as insiders, will have opinions to convey. One way to look at this is: What should the new leader start doing, stop doing, avoid doing and keep doing? Peers will have specific needs of the new leader pertaining to their own operations' effectiveness and continuity. These needs must be identified.

The consultant must also keep in mind that it is often a new leader's peers who can be the most career impacting. Bosses tend to allow subordinates some breathing room for a while. Direct reports are typically apprehensive when a new leader is assigned. They work for the new leader and will be more directly affected by the change. Peers, on the other hand, because they stand to be either positively or negatively impacted by the new leader in relation to their mutual boss, tend to be the most critical when things are not going well and conversely are complimentary when things are going well. In short, this is a very important set of interviews that will be discussed in more detail in chapter six.

Direct Reports Interviews

The third segment to be interviewed are the new leader's direct reports—ALL of them—from the next ranking manager to the administrative assistant. This group is naturally a bit apprehensive about changing leaders, even if they were looking forward to getting a new boss. Change is disruptive, and there is a natural tendency for direct reports to be a bit skeptical about how things will ultimately work out after a new boss arrives. Furthermore, each of them has individual concerns to some degree. Perhaps their promotion track was tied directly (and positively) to a former boss. They may have personal situations that were well understood by the previous boss that will need to be explained to their new boss early in the transition (which is awkward at best). Perhaps, there are uncertainties about future evaluations and how to communicate effectively with their new boss. Does the new leader prefer face-to-face meetings? Or emails? Or phone calls? Does he or she drop in unannounced? Does the new leader want to have standing appointments with each direct report? Or would he or she prefer for direct reports to initiate any one-on-one meetings? All such questions need answers as early as possible.

There are many details direct reports know about the new leader's job that need to be captured in this process. They also know the history of the organization and what actions and policies have succeeded in the past and why. An overarching objective of focusing so much attention on the direct reports is that the communication barriers and lack of trust that naturally exist during a transition can be eliminated right away. If the new leader's team quickly gets the impression that they are dealing with an authentic, transparent and approachable individual, they will more readily contribute freely in the beginning rather than taking a "wait and see" attitude that could take weeks or months, if ever, to end.

Documentation

The consultant will likely have interviewed 12 or more individuals—boss (or board members), peers and direct reports. A compilation of sample questions is found at <u>Appendix B</u>. *The consultant may want to add to or delete questions from this list.* Regardless, there will have been a great deal of meaningful information gathered—all of it critical to the new leader's short-term success. The project must continue to move along at a brisk pace because the start date is usually not far off (two to four weeks from the acceptance of an offer is the norm for a new hire—often less time for an internal promotion or transfer).

Once the interviews are complete, the consultant must rapidly document everything. This document will vary in length based on the amount of information the consultant was able to gather. It is structured in such a way that it will become the new leader's "blueprint for success" once compiled. It is organized from the top down. First, input from the boss or board is presented, then the peers and finally, the direct reports. On those occasions where other stakeholders may be part of the process, for example, a key customer (or two or three), a key supplier, etc., their information is presented last. Regardless, the document is usually a substantial one. It is important that it be organized in such a way that the information contained within it can easily be absorbed by the new leader. A suggested format for this document is at Appendix C.

It will likely take the consultant a couple of days to write this document. Once finished, it is provided to the new leader either in a hard copy, PDF format, or both. The heading of the report should be marked "CONFIDENTIAL." The message to convey is that there are only two copies: the new leader's copy and the consultant's working copy. Routinely, these reports reflect candid comments that would not otherwise have been captured had the consultant not made it clear that the responses to questions would be for the new leader's eyes only. It should be noted, however, that some information gathered may be too sensitive to appear in a document of this kind. The consultant must assure the responder that such input will be discussed with the new leader but not documented. Otherwise, the consultant must use professional discretion at all times as to what should be documented and what should not.

Once the document is completed, the new leader needs to receive it as soon as possible. The next step is for the new leader to thoroughly review the information contained within it. It is this blueprint that will guide the new leader in doing the right things sooner (and avoiding the wrong things, altogether) in the first few weeks and months on the job.

Debriefing

The debriefing process is the most critical phase of the new leader integration project. The consultant and the new leader meet one-on-one for what will often be a day-long meeting to review the document that the consultant prepared. Since the new leader will be in transition and possibly dealing with a family move and all the hectic activity associated with relocating, it would be best for the consultant to travel to the new leader's location. There are those who think this meeting can be accomplished adequately via Skype or some other videoconferencing capability, and that is not without merit, but if at all possible, this meeting should occur face-to-face.

The new leader will have studied the document and made notes. The consultant will have a working copy as well. At the beginning of the meeting the consultant will review the overall document, highlighting the major points that need to be emphasized. Throughout this meeting the new leader will be asking a myriad of questions. One of the advantages to having a process consultant oversee this integration effort is that the consultant will have the most current view of the organization and all of the stakeholders who will be in the new leader's sphere of influence. The consultant will know what needs to be stressed and also where the potential issues lie. If others, such as key clients, suppliers, etc., have been part of the process, the consultant will have the details of those discussions as well. All of this valuable information needs to be well understood and organized by the consultant in order to be communicated clearly to the new leader.

The main objective of the debriefing is to refine the blueprint for what the new leader will be expected to do and avoid doing during the first weeks and months, including the first day on the job. The debriefing reinforces what needs to be accomplished from at least three dimensions—boss, peers and direct reports. It also provides the new leader with the insights of an experienced change management consultant. The first 90 days are critical to the success of the new leader. This document and the debriefing will pay great dividends, assuming, of course, that the best person for the job was recruited and hired in the first place and the right consultant was appointed or retained to guide the new leader through the integration process.

There is another key objective for this debriefing and that is: to prepare the new leader for the kick-off meeting that will occur during the new leader's first day at work. And that is the topic of the next phase.

Kick-off Meeting

If there is a step in the process that can cause some concern on the part of the incoming leader, it is the kick-off meeting on the first day. Think back to some of your own transitions. You wanted to be in control of that first meeting with the people who reported to you, and this process takes away some of that control. It is critical, therefore, that the boss let the new leader know ahead of time how much value will come from this process and how much the organization supports it. In fact, the organization must OWN the process, not just support it, for the New Leader Integration to work most effectively.

During the New Leader Integration process, the direct reports disclose what they perceive are the actions most needing attention. They also have questions and possible concerns about their new leader that need to be addressed early in the process. They are most interested in determining what this leadership change will do for them as a group and as individuals. Let's face it: getting a new boss is stressful even if the team was glad to see the predecessor go. This meeting, therefore, is a golden opportunity for the new leader to get off to a great start, which is why so much preparation goes into it. Otherwise, what would likely occur in the absence of this intervention would be that the meeting, whenever it happened, would be left to chance. The team would be slower to disclose information openly until trust developed (if ever) and would have no idea what the new leader's priorities are and how to best communicate with that individual until days or weeks later.

An hour into this meeting many of these concerns will have begun to evaporate, which is a big reason why the meeting is prepared for in such detail and facilitated by a change management consultant. During the second half of the meeting, the direct reports will openly discuss some key issues and actions needed with their new boss, and trust and confidence will be developing much more quickly than if left to happen on its own. The more the direct reports know about their new leader and the key short-term objectives he or she has received from the top, the sooner they can effectively get down to business with their new boss without the typical transition distractions.

A consultant facilitates this meeting for many reasons. By that point in the process, every member of the new leader's team will have met the consultant and shared a great deal of information. If the consultant has operated effectively, the direct reports will be very hopeful that this process will, indeed, make a meaningful difference, and they will come to the meeting with an open mind and a positive attitude. The new leader will arrive energized as well.

As the saying goes, "Knowledge is power." Few leaders have the good fortune to enter a new position so well prepared... knowing so much, so soon. Remember that this process took place for the most part before the start date and involved a minimal time commitment on the part of the new leader in transition, leading up to this kick-off meeting. It is a win-win event, and it results in a team that is off and running the first day, addressing issues before the meeting ends. This is a confidence builder for the direct reports as well as for the new leader.

The consultant will have spent time with the new leader during the document debriefing session (and afterwards, if necessary) to thoroughly prepare for this important meeting.

Follow-Up

This phase is the step in the process with the most flexibility and can be accomplished in several ways. One way—the most productive way—is for the consultant to stay in touch and to meet with the new leader and his or her boss at the 30, 60 and 90 day points. These are check-in meetings where the boss's input to the blueprint becomes the talking points. A boss who has contributed to this process with confidence knows that these structured check-in meetings are of great value and can only improve outcomes. The consultant helps to shape the meetings and ensures the right things are addressed.

If for some reason the new leader's boss is not part of the follow-up phase, another option is for the consultant to stay in contact and check in with the new leader at 30, 60 and 90 day intervals. Using the entire blueprint as a talking paper, these meetings are held to assist the new leader in staying focused. An effective consultant will act as a sounding board, so the check-in sessions, in essence, are executive coaching sessions to some degree.

Another option is only viable if the organization has a formal executive coaching process for new leaders. If they do, the executive coach should be briefed by the consultant and the new leader about what has transpired to date and what lies ahead in the short-term. The coach can then assist the new leader as he or she continues the integration process. While this is an excellent approach, few organizations currently assign coaches to newly hired executives. An option would be to have the New Leader Integration process consultant continue on in this role beyond the first 90 days for up to a year.

What to Do if a New Leader Integration Process is Unavailable to You

If you are reading this book as a soon-to-be new leader, and the organization you are joining has not yet made a commitment to a comprehensive New Leader Integration program, you are probably asking yourself what you can do to improve the effectiveness of your own integration. There are some questions within this book which could be appropriate for you to ask your stakeholders early in the hiring process or your tenure as new leader. If you have been recruited by an executive search firm, the recruiter who is working with you could be a good person to ask some of these questions for you and get back to you with answers. Which questions to ask (and when…and to whom) is a judgment call. A compilation of questions from which to choose is at Appendix B.

In addition to the value of the questions posed in this book, there are several other books that specifically guide new leaders in transition. These books outline a self-directed integration process that occurs for the most part after the start date. The emphasis here is on "self-directed." There are two that are well known. They are: *The New Leader's 100-Day Action Plan (Second Edition)—How to Take Charge, Build Your Team, and Get Immediate Results*, by George B. Bradt, Jayme A. Check and Jorge E. Pedraza, published by John Wiley & Sons; and *The First 90 Days—Critical Success Strategies for New Leaders at All Levels*, by Michael Watkins, published by Harvard Business School Press.

CHAPTER 3

Moving Up or Over: Integrating Internal Leader Promotions and Transfers

U p to this point, we have focused on a New Leader Integration process for managers hired from the outside. However, many leader changes are not the result of outside recruiting activity. Instead, they result from internal promotions or cross-divisional or cross-functional reassignments, such as when a sales executive becomes a general manager, or when a marketing executive is given responsibility for sales as well. These internal leadership changes are statistically more likely to be successful for an organization than outside hires (although, as the research shows, not by much). An insider knows the pluses and minuses of the organization's culture—its past wins, losses and mistakes, the reasons why (in many cases), and the quirks and strengths of its leaders. This is hard-won knowledge for an outsider and in some cases can come too late to make a difference.

Those are the upsides of internal promotions or transfers. One of the downsides is that almost everyone on the management team knows something already, both positive and negative, about a new leader who has moved from within the organization, or if they do not know already, that information is easy to obtain. Occasionally, there are hard feelings when one individual is promoted over others. In addition, an internal new leader may already have opinions about what needs to be done and perceptions regarding who (rightly or wrongly) is an asset and who is a liability. Such is not the case with an outside hire. You can see the trade offs, and we have all seen them manifested in the organizations to which we have been assigned.

The New Leader Integration process is also effective for an internally promoted or reassigned executive. The most notable challenge facing this transition, however, is the fact that when an internal promotion occurs, the incoming leader often has only a few days to make the transition. More often than not, there is no relocation involved, but even if there is, the new leader is leaving one job in the organization and assuming responsibility for another. It is common to see the new leader have difficulty completely severing from a former job before assuming new responsibilities. This overlap of duties can sometimes go on for days or weeks. The consultant is able to gather the important information needed by the new leader while this awkward transition is underway. If the consultant is an internal resource as well (e.g., a director or

VP of organization development), a trust factor may already exist that can be leveraged. This is a very different dynamic than when an outside executive joins an organization.

Does the basic process methodology change? Not really. The consultant will interview the same groups of stakeholders, gather the same information in confidence, compile the same information succinctly, and meet with the new leader to provide the same insights as would otherwise have happened for an outside hire. In many cases, the difference is that less of the information captured and presented will be a big surprise to the internal leader who is moving up or over. The kick-off meeting on the new leader's first day is equally as important for an internally promoted new leader. It builds trust (or strengthens it) through the answering of people's questions upfront. It also reinforces that the new leader is now well-informed, and everyone can get on with their duties and responsibilities with minimal disruptions and angst.

The transitional follow-up meetings with the new leader, boss and consultant are also important for internally promoted executives.

CHAPTER 4

Choosing the Right New Leader Integration Process Consultant

There are a variety of resources from which an organization can draw to facilitate this New Leader Integration pre-boarding process. What are some of them?

Internal Consultant

If your organization has a director or vice president of organization development, that individual may be well-qualified to oversee this process, and would be appropriate for both outside hires and internal promotions. Most OD executives are experienced in a variety of change management techniques. Other organizations might have the senior human resources executive perform the New Leader Integration process, or another mid-level HR executive with a talent for this type of work. If qualified, any of these individuals would be perceived by an incoming new leader as having functional responsibility for executive transitions.

If your organization elects to assign an internal resource to conduct a New Leader Integration process, the individual you choose will need to participate in the interview cycle of all candidates. The internal consultant would be able to get to know the candidates in advance of a hire, explain to each candidate the details of the New Leader Integration process and the role the OD or HR executive would play in the process, and better understand why the new leader was hired instead of other candidates who were being considered. A by-product of this involvement is that the internal consultant could also gauge the receptivity of the potential new hires with respect to participating in a New Leader Integration process, which could be valuable feedback as a hiring decision draws to a close.

What organizations need to avoid is thrusting a process consultant on the new leader at the last minute, unannounced and previously unmet. In short, ensure that your internal consultant gets to know the candidate before a hiring decision is made. Being part of the interview cycle with all candidates is an excellent way to accomplish this.

External Consultant

In the absence of internal resources to do this work, there are many outside OD or change management consultants, many of whom are in private practice, who could conduct this process for you if provided an outline of your expectations and the process you want them to follow. They may have ideas of their own to offer to enhance the process. Nonetheless, an outside consultant would also need to be assigned early in the hiring phase and interview each candidate on the "short list." Whether the consultant is an internal one or an external one, there is no substitute for the new leader and consultant knowing one another in advance of offer acceptance so that the new leader knows what to expect in the immediate days ahead.

An effective way to secure the services of outside consultants would be to develop a Request for Proposal (RFP) to which interested consultants could respond. The integration process is far too important to limit the pool of consultants to a given geography, but if there are experienced consultants already in your city or region, it does make it more convenient to conduct a fast-paced leader integration process if they are already in the vicinity.

Ideally, an organization would have a "pool" of good process consultants from which to draw. This is critical for the simple reason that New Leader Integration almost always happens on short notice. A search may have been underway for months, and the selection process may have been moving slowly when suddenly an offer is extended and accepted. The new leader is anywhere from two to four weeks away from arriving and is anxious to get to work in the new job. If you do not have a pool of consultants to provide this service, you might easily find yourself in a situation where no one is available to integrate your new leader (assuming you have to go outside of your organization for this service). Good consultants are always busy, and there is a high likelihood that your need and their schedules may not match. Therefore the more consultants you have in your pool the better.

One global organization uses a similar process for executive coaching. They have one organization development consulting firm that oversees their global executive coaching effort. This firm identifies and qualifies other coaches on a regional or national basis who can serve as a resource, as needed. They have several from which to choose at all times in order to ensure that an executive coach is always available on short notice.

Should you choose to rely on internal resources to provide a New Leader Integration service for you, keep in mind that those individuals may already be fully committed to other important projects that cannot be interrupted when a New Leader Integration need arises. For that reason it is best, even if you would prefer to have just internal consultants serve in this role, that you secure some external consulting talent. That way you will have the depth of resources you need to ensure you are never left short-handed with a New Leader Integration requirement.

The same pressures exist with internal promotions or transfers. These, too, can often occur on short notice. If so, consultant resources could be in short supply if you have not acted in advance to build a pool of them.

Assuming you have fully committed your organization to providing integration support to all new leaders, this pool of consultant resources should all be "tested under fire" in order to determine the most effective consultants. Also, you will eventually come to the conclusion that some consultants are better suited to work with certain individuals. Advance planning and consultant scouting and recruiting can carry you a long way toward implementing an effective New Leader Integration program.

If your organization is globally distributed, it would be more effective if your pool of consultants were also from the appropriate country or region. It is helpful if the new leader and the other people involved in the process have a cultural comfort level with the process consultant. In short, "fit" matters. Try to match the consultant with the new leader and the stakeholders whenever possible.

Executive Recruiter

Who else could provide this service to you? If the new leader is an outside hire who has come to you through an executive recruiting firm, the search consultant could be in a good position to facilitate this process. The recruiter is already adept at fact finding and interviewing a wide variety of people. The recruiter would have already gathered a great deal of information about the organization, including the track record of the predecessor in the position, who the major players are, and how people view the previous leader and the organization in general. The search consultant will usually know the candidate better than anyone in the hiring organization to this point. The executive recruiter, having personally conducted references on the new leader, knows the candidate's strengths and weaknesses and also knows the other candidates who were evaluated, and what made the new leader click with the hiring executives from the organization. Finally, if the search went well, there is a high degree of trust already existing between the new leader and the search consultant. After all, it is the executive recruiter who made this new opportunity possible and helped the new leader to navigate the hiring process, up to and often including playing a key role in negotiating the compensation package.

It is likely, however, that most executive recruiters will have little to no interest in providing this level of service. Historically, recruiters view their work as finished the day an offer is accepted (or the start date). Some follow the new hire through the first month or so to ensure that no major unexpected issues arise. A New Leader Integration service is outside the paradigm of many executive recruiters. It is a point worth discussing with your executive search consultant at an appropriate time. Is this a service that the recruiter's firm would willingly provide? It could be. However, organizations should expect to pay an additional fee (on top of the search retainer) for this service if a search firm performs it.

PART II

THE NEW LEADER INTEGRATION PROCESS

CHAPTER 5

The Boss (or Board) Interview

I n the interview phase with the boss or board, it is important that the consultant first gather some general information before getting down to specifics. One must not assume that the new leader gathered much of this general information earlier during the hiring process.

In this stage, the consultant interviews the boss or key board member(s). A sample list of questions to ask includes the following:

General Information

How would you describe the culture of the organization?

The answer to this question should be compared with the answers of peers and direct reports who will also be asked the same question. The new leader needs to know how the organization's top executive or the new leader's immediate boss views the culture of the organization. Probe a bit. Ask why the culture is that way. Why is it important? Does the organization's success or failures have anything to do with the current culture? Does the boss or board want to see the culture of the new leader's organization change? If yes, how should it change and in what timeframe? Why is that important?

What type of executive fits in well at this organization?

The answer to this question sets the tone for the incoming leader as to the degree of importance the boss or board places on certain leadership and managerial traits, aptitudes, competencies and style. For example, if the boss is a no-nonsense, get-right-to-the-point type of person, then the new leader needs to know right away that communicating with the boss must be well-ordered and succinct, both when meeting one-on-one and in written communication.

One boss acted as though every impromptu meeting was an unwelcomed interruption. The new leader knew this in advance and would preface every such encounter with the words, "I know you're busy. This will just take a minute." The boss's body language would change from one of, "Oh, not another interruption!" to one of openness and receptivity. The new leader had established a contract of sorts with the boss: If you will hear me out, I promise not to waste your time. The new leader always ensured that he was organized and succinct in all face-to-face communications with the boss. If the discussion began to take on more of the boss's time than planned, the new leader would interrupt and state that he had promised this would "just take a minute" and it was obviously taking more time. He would then offer to come back at a more convenient time to finish the discussion. The boss usually invited him to remain, and sometimes the discussion would run on for a half hour or so. But the contract had not been broken. The new leader gave the boss the option of continuing or stopping the meeting, which was noted…and appreciated.

This kind of information is powerful to know in advance. During the job interviews it may not be readily apparent as to how to best communicate with the boss in day-to-day working situations. This question is also asked of the peer group to provide another point of view.

What type of executive does NOT fit in well at this organization?

This is the other side of the coin. The boss will let the consultant know in no uncertain terms which leadership styles and practices work best in the organization and which ones do not. There will usually be no names associated with this answer, but the information is valuable for the new leader nonetheless. This information will not likely have been available to the new leader during the hiring process. If the new leader is already a member of the organization, this question may seem to have an apparent answer, but if the individual is moving from one division to another, the answer to that question may vary widely between the two division chiefs. A new leader from within the organization should assume that when a boss changes, everything changes, until proven otherwise. This, too, is also a good question to ask the peer group for cross-referencing.

What problems or hurdles has the organization faced in the past two years?

In a recruiting situation this type of information is often glossed over or kept close to the vest. Once onboard, however, a new leader will soon discover the specific challenges the organization has faced and why. There are many reasons why bosses contain this information during the hiring process. The most obvious reason is if the new leader is coming from, or may end up with, a competitor. The boss will not want to share this information until the new leader is onboard. Once an offer is accepted, it is a good time to answer this question in detail.

What problems or hurdles has the new leader's department faced in the past two years?

As with questions about the organization in general, some of this information may have been shared with the new leader during the hiring process. Now that the new leader is onboard, it is OK to share the full story. Bosses always have an answer to questions concerning prior problems and hurdles. The fact that a new leader has been hired may be an indication that all was not rosy in the new leader's department or division.

What are your most important values?

The candidate might have asked this question during the job interview but rarely does, so it is an important question for the consultant to ask. The answer will speak volumes to the new leader about the boss's worldview.

What sets this organization apart from the competition?

If the new leader were recruited away from the competition, this information would likely not have been fully disclosed during the hiring process. Now that the new leader has been hired and is soon to be onboard, these insights need to be shared.

What rumors, good or bad, exist in the marketplace pertaining to your organization?

Unless the new leader is coming directly from a competitor, it is difficult to know the answer to this question unless it is available in the press or on the Internet—which is often the case. Nonetheless, it is time to share with the new leader what is being said about the organization.

How would you describe your management team?

A hidden part of this question is in essence, "How does the management team work together?" The answer allows the new leader to know what the boss likes and dislikes about the management team's interactions with one another and with him or her. It is not unusual for the new leader to be the only member of the management team that fully understands the boss's thinking on this subject, mainly because no one else prior to the consultant has ever asked the question so directly. When asked, bosses will generally be forthcoming with a very informative answer.

What worked well for the predecessor in the job (and not so well)?

It would stand to reason that the candidate would have asked this question during the job interviews, but that is rarely the case. What recruiters routinely hear candidates ask is, "Why is this position open?" or "What happened to the last person in the job?" That is not the same as asking what the predecessor did well and not so well. The questions recruiters hear are aimed at helping candidates determine whether they want to compete for a given executive opportunity, but the question the consultant is asking will specifically benefit the new leader in the integration process. It is a sensitive question, especially if the predecessor remains within the organization (even if promoted). But it is a fair question to ask, and when asked, is generally answered tactfully but informatively.

What was the background of the last person in the position?

This may or may not be known by the new leader. Assume it is not and ask the question. The answer will go a long way toward helping the new leader appreciate some of the reasons why the predecessor was successful or unsuccessful.

What was lacking in the background/skill-set of the last person in the position?

If the boss is willing to answer this question, it will assist the new leader greatly in identifying skill deficits that may require an investment in some self-directed personal development.

How do you see the current business situation (Turnaround? Sustainment? Other?)

Each situation communicates a different mindset and management approach for the new leader. It is very likely that this would have been covered in the interview process, but if not, it needs to be addressed here. In the case of an internal transfer or promotion, it may not be obvious to the incoming leader what the exact situation is perceived to be in the eyes of the boss. The new leader's plans and actions need to address the appropriate business situation.

Specific Questions

How do you want the new leader to communicate with you?

Bosses have varying communication styles to say the least. Some do not want face-to-face meetings unless they initiate them. Others invite their direct reports to have a periodic one-on-one meeting with them on a weekly or bi-weekly basis. These meetings run the gamut from being highly structured to highly unstructured. They can be scheduled for precision, right down to the minute, or more open-ended. It is important for the new leader to know quickly how the boss's direct reports communicate in person (as well as in staff meetings).

Equally important are all the in-between communication events. In one organization the boss preferred email as the primary means of communication and agreed to face-to-face meetings sparingly. He sent emails out to the organization's managers, even if they reported to other managers, and expected prompt replies. The introduction of the BlackBerry made this practice even more onerous, as he expected all members of the management team to have their BlackBerry devices on at all times. He rarely took phone calls or made them. Email was his tool. Everyone in the interview process alerted potential newcomers to this leader's communication preference in advance of accepting a job offer. It worked for the boss, and he received prompt responses to his emails. His management team, however, had to compensate for his out-of-the-ordinary communication channels. The point here is not to debate the pros and cons of this communication style. Suffice it to say, had new leaders coming into this organization not been aware of this practice and reacted negatively to it, they would have run the risk of failure in their positions.

How frequently do you want the new leader to communicate with you and in what level of detail?

Aside from the specific details about how best to communicate with the boss, there is information the boss will want to know on a regular basis, the subject matter of which may be standard and repetitive, and often takes the form of weekly or monthly status reports or updates. What is the boss looking for in these reports? How do others write them? How much detail does each team member provide and what format do they use? It is the type of information best obtained in advance rather than under pressure once onboard.

What types of issues/decisions require consultation with you in advance?

These decisions can range from expenditures above a certain amount, needed items that were not in the budget, terminations, other disciplinary actions, or any number of things. No new leader wants to overstep boundaries. As much guidance from the boss that can be obtained on this topic in advance of the start date, the better off the new leader will be.

How will the new leader's performance be measured?

The higher the position of the new leader, the more likely it is that these types of details will be covered somewhat in the hiring process. This is due in large part to the fact that for high level positions, incentive compensation is usually tied to specific performance criteria, and those details may have been spelled out in the offer letter. However, not all managers know this in advance. While performance objectives can often be fluid documents changing from year to year, generally speaking, a boss knows what is expected of direct reports and can respond to this question with some specificity. The boss and the new leader will eventually work this out, but the more the new leader knows about performance measurement criteria going into the new job, the more those expectations can be incorporated into day-to-day activities right from the start.

What factors (soft and hard) make the new leader's business situation a challenge?

It is very useful to know how challenges evolved before knowing specifically what the new leader will need to address.

In most cases, a boss (or board) will have a growing list of what specific challenges exist in a new leader's organization and will have been waiting to fill the position in order to finally see them addressed. That does not mean, however, that this information has been consolidated and documented for the new leader. These challenges are the boss or board's "hot buttons" and need to be identified and communicated.

What specific projects need attention in the first 30, 60 and 90 days?

The answers to this question will be the anchor of the process where the boss or board is concerned. While the new leader's peers and direct reports will be asked a similar question, the new leader will need to accept that input from them in relation to what the boss clearly expects. Occasionally, there is a direct contradiction between what the direct reports think should be the focus and what the boss or board thinks should be emphasized. Knowing this in advance of the start date is critical. How the new leader interacts with others in the first days and weeks will need to be tempered by what the boss said in response to this question.

It is important for the consultant to spend an appropriate amount of time on this question and leave with clearly defined answers. There will not be a second chance to capture this information. In the debriefing session with the new leader, the consultant will need to point out any disagreements that exist among each stakeholder's answers to this question. If there are conflicting answers, point these out clearly to the new leader. If there is unanimity from the group, that, too, is very important for the new leader to know.

The guidance the new leader receives in this answer will be the cornerstone to the periodic meetings the consultant will later facilitate with the new leader and boss on a monthly basis through the first 90 days.

What will constitute the "must happens" in the first 90 days?

In the final analysis, the boss will want to see the new leader score points quickly in relation to several key tasks that rise above the others. What are they?

How do you view the new leader's team of people?

This question will also be asked of the peers. Their answers, when compared to the boss's answer, will be very informative. The new leader may be expected to assess the team and respond accordingly to the boss within the first 90 days. This is a potential issue for the new leader, especially, for example, if the boss is displeased with the team and the new leader later finds them to be superlative now that they have new direction.

What should the new leader avoid (specific, known or potential pitfalls)?

There are pitfalls in every organization that are to be avoided, and some to be avoided at all costs. Problems may pertain to key customers, key suppliers, a certain board member, the media, etc. It is human nature that one major mistake can negate the value of several early wins. So what must be avoided? This question will be asked of all participants in the process. Differing perspectives on their answers will be very enlightening to the new leader.

What key resources are available or soon will be available or are unavailable and will remain unavailable?

What are the essential resources that the new leader can expect from the boss? What did the previous leader in that role want? Were those resources forthcoming? Will any of these resources soon be available? Are there resources that the previous leader wanted that will never be available? Is this negotiable?

What do you want to see done the same way as the new leader's predecessor?

As the saying goes, "Even a stopped clock is right twice a day." There were certain things the previous leader did that the boss liked, even if the previous leader had ultimately been unsuccessful. What were they? Why was this important to the boss? How important is it that the new leader continues to do those things in that way?

What do you want to see done differently from the new leader's predecessor?

It could be anything ranging from a time wasting practice to a consistent method of dealing with conflict or decision-making that displeased the boss. Determine as many of these things as possible. This is valuable information for the new leader.

The Boss (or Board) Sample Interview Questions

General Questions

1. How would you describe the culture of the organization?
2. What type of executive fits in well at this organization?
3. What type of executive does NOT fit in well at this organization?
4. What problems or hurdles has the organization faced in the past two years?
5. What problems or hurdles has the new leader's department faced in the past two years?
6. What are your most important values?
7. What sets this organization apart from the competition?
8. What rumors, good or bad, exist in the marketplace pertaining to your organization?
9. How would you describe your management team?
10. What worked well for the predecessor in the job (and not so well)?
11. What was the background of the last person in the position?
12. What was lacking in the background/skill set of the last person in the position?
13. How do you see the current business situation (Turnaround? Sustainment? Other?)

Specific Questions

14. How do you want the new leader to communicate with you (What medium?)?

15. How frequently do you want the new leader to communicate with you (and in what level of detail)?
16. What types of issues and decisions require consultation with you in advance?
17. How will the new leader's performance be measured?
18. What factors (soft and hard) make the new leader's business situation a challenge?
19. What specific projects need attention in the first 30, 60 and 90 days?
20. What will constitute the "must happens" in the first 90 days?
21. How do you view the new leader's team of people?
22. What should the new leader avoid (specific, known or potential pitfalls)?
23. What key resources are available to the new leader or soon will be available or are unavailable and will remain unavailable?
24. What do you want to see done in the same way as the new leader's predecessor?
25. What do you want to see done differently from the new leader's predecessor?

CHAPTER 6

The Peer Group Interviews

In some way or another, it is important how each executive operates. The success or failure, the efficiency or inefficiency, of each member of the management team matters. For that reason it is important for the consultant to spend time with each of the new leader's peers. In most situations they will be specialists of one sort of another (e.g., finance, HR, sales, marketing, supply chain, etc.). Each of them will have an opinion as to how well or poorly the new leader's predecessor performed. In every case the peers will have opinions as to how that individual made their jobs easier or harder to perform and what they would like to see the new leader do the same as or differently than the predecessor.

In some situations the new leader's predecessor will have remained with the organization in a new role that is either a move up or a move over, so their responses to some questions may be tentative. Each time the consultant conducts an interview, he or she will need to emphasize what the process is, how it is being conducted and what the desired outcomes are. While the information may be sensitive, each respondent needs to determine how important that information would be to the new leader and share it accordingly.

There are fewer questions that will be asked of the new leader's peer group than was asked of the boss. Here is a sample list of questions to ask:

How would you describe the culture of the organization?

This question was also asked of the boss. It is important to hear what each peer has to say about the culture of the organization. This information will need to be cross-referenced with the boss's and direct reports' comments in the report provided to the new leader.

What type of executive fits in at this organization?

This question, too, was asked of the boss. Each peer will have a unique answer. The objective here is to validate what the boss had to say, or to point out to the new leader that there are significant discrepancies that exist between the boss's view and the peers' views.

What type of executive does NOT fit in at this organization?

The boss will have had definite opinions in response to this question. Do the peers share similar opinions? Where do they agree? How do they differ?

From your perspective, what should the new leader focus on in the first 30, 60 and 90 days?

The peers' answers to this question should be in concert with those given by the boss or board and the direct reports. Note any differences of opinion. Peers have some knowledge of what is working and not working in the new leader's area of operation and should be able to provide some valuable insights.

The consultant should expect to hear functionally-specific guidance coming from the peers. For example, the CFO would know that budgets are soon due, and the previous leader may have had some difficulty with one aspect of the budget in the preparation phase—a misstep that made the CFO's job more difficult. In a case such as that, the consultant could expect to hear some specific guidance that would hopefully ensure that the issue is not repeated.

The HR executive would know of a pending downsizing or the launch of an organization-wide training program that will impact the new leader's staff.

A marketing executive would know that the new leader's department will be involved in a new product launch that will require the new leader's assistance.

The CIO may need to share that there will be a major upgrade in the organization's enterprise software in the near future which will especially impact the new leader's operation.

The supply chain executive may be facing the expansion of a well-running distribution system from a national to a global operation and that move will impact the new leader's organization.

The point here is that there are specific, functionally-related, tasks and projects that are almost always underway that are the responsibility of a new leader's peers. The more that can be known about events that will happen in 30 day increments over the course of the first 90 days, the more useful this information will be to the incoming leader. It is appropriate to go out beyond 90 days if the peer knows of other significant events that will directly impact upon the new leader.

What does the new leader need to do to ensure your own continued effectiveness?

This is a personal question. It can be something as simple as "Return my phone calls!" to ensuring that input from the new leader (such as budget numbers) be done on time.

What does the new leader need to avoid doing to ensure your own effectiveness?

What the consultant is looking for here are potential problem areas. It could be something along the lines of the predecessor's history of undermining the peer's ability to operate effectively and efficiently. The peer may have led an ad-hoc task force that needed people from the new leader's organization. In the past the previous leader may have avoided assigning the appropriate people, and this decision may have impacted the outcome of the peer's project. There could be several answers to this question. The consultant will need to continue to probe until the list is exhausted.

What do you want the new leader to continue to do that the predecessor did?

A good management team knows the strengths and weaknesses of each member. They come to depend upon each other in a variety of ways they often take for granted. This question is aimed at helping the peer recall examples where the previous leader excelled at his or her job. While every new leader intends to make a personal mark on the organization, it stands to reason that if a peer were particularly pleased with what the predecessor routinely did in certain situations, the hope would be that the new leader would continue to do likewise. Through this question, the peer can isolate those positive behaviors or services that worked in the past.

What do you want the new leader to stop doing that the predecessor did?

Here is another opportunity for the peer to identify what could potentially be improved. It could be that the predecessor was habitually late to staff meetings and the boss was overly patient, thus making everyone have to wait until that person arrived in order to start the meeting. This is an opportune time for the peer to attempt to set the stage for positive change with the introduction of a new leader.

What do you want the new leader to start doing that the predecessor did not do?

This question provides the opportunity for the peer to ask for a service or behavior that will improve the peer's operation. It might be something as simple as to include a member of the peer's organization in certain meetings to ensure a proper coordination effort.

From your perspective, how best is it to communicate with the boss (e.g., style, techniques)?

The peer will likely have figured this out already. The boss may not want issues brought up in routine staff meetings and instead wants issues saved for other meetings. The peer may know that the boss does not read anything over a page in length so the new leader should learn quickly to be succinct in written communication. It may be that the peer can read the boss's body language and can thus coach the new leader on how best to reason with the boss (or avoid reasoning) when the boss is frustrated about something. Whatever the peer knows about communicating with the boss will carry the new leader far and ensure a positive working relationship. Probe deeply when asking this question.

How do you want the new leader to communicate with you?

This is the time to let the new leader know, for example, that the peer depends on email almost to the exclusion of any other means of communication, that phone calls will always go into voice mail and that responses to voice mail will usually come through emails or text messages unless it is absolutely necessary to have a phone conversation. The peer may be someone who will always walk down the hallway and "drop in" to get an answer rather than email or call.

How do you generally and specifically view the new leader's staff?

Unless there was a major issue between the peer and the predecessor's staff, this question is likely to receive a tactful response. Assuming that is the case, the consultant needs to probe. The new leader needs to be aware of any conflict between a peer and a member of the new leader's staff. More often the conflict may be between one of the peer's key staff members and one of the new leader's staff members. Helping to resolve such a problem early can carry a new leader a long way in the eyes of a peer who is looking for some immediate, positive relief to occur as part of this leadership change.

What should the new leader avoid doing at all costs?

This question will cause the peer to think about events or behaviors that have raised the ire of the boss or other peers in the past. For example, "Never initiate a conversation with a board member without the boss knowing about it in advance." Every organization has its absolute no-no's. If the peer can share some of them, the new leader will be much better off and have a higher likelihood of avoiding mistakes. These lessons are hard-won and the peer would hopefully practice the "Golden Rule" to, "Do unto others as you would have them do unto you."

The Peer Group Sample Interview Questions

1. How would you describe the culture of the organization?

2. What type of executive fits in at this organization?

3. What type of executive does NOT fit in at this organization?

4. From your perspective, what should the new leader focus on in the first 30, 60 and 90 days?

5. What does the new leader need to do to ensure your own continued effectiveness?

6. What does the new leader need to avoid doing to ensure your own effectiveness?

7. What do you want the new leader to continue to do that the predecessor did?

8. What do you want the new leader to stop doing that the predecessor did?

9. What do you want the new leader to start doing that the predecessor did not do?

10. From your perspective, how best is it to communicate with the boss (e.g., style, technique)?

11. How do you want the new leader to communicate with you?

12. How do you generally and specifically view the new leader's staff?

13. What should the new leader avoid doing at all costs?

CHAPTER 7

The Direct Reports Interviews

Most new leaders are pulled in two directions upon assuming a new position: meeting the boss's expectations and ensuring that the people they lead accept them quickly and work together toward common goals. While it is easier to focus on meeting the expectations of the boss, a team of direct reports has diverse goals, perspectives, biases, concerns, questions and needs that must collectively be addressed. Every experienced leader understands what it is like to have been the direct report to a new boss as well as having been the new boss. What actually happens in the initial days of a transition endures. If the integration process goes well in the first days and weeks, it is more likely that the new leader's follow-on initiatives will be better supported.

Employing sound leadership principles and practices is vital in new leader transitions. Leadership is an influencing process. Since communication is the medium of leadership, it must flow smoothly in both directions. For a new leader to integrate quickly and effectively, initial communication must be a positive experience for the direct reports. The goal is to gain their trust and quickly establish open communication. We all look for authenticity and transparency in our leaders, whatever the level. Candor is essential. Direct reports will size up their new leader quickly, which supports the old adage, "You only have one opportunity to make a good first impression." It is essential, therefore, that the new leader end the first day on the job by having left a positive impression on those being led as it will continue to pay dividends. The New Leader Integration process improves the likelihood that this first encounter will be a positive one. It is important to the new leader's ultimate success (both short and long-term) that a great deal of attention be placed on the direct reports.

The consultant will interview each of the new leader's direct reports. Most of the questions will focus on their perspectives, opinions, experience, concerns, issues and questions. In addition, they will be asked some of the questions that were previously directed to the new leader's boss and peers. The consultant needs to inform each individual that on the new leader's start date, there will be a meeting with the direct reports hosted by their new leader and facilitated by the consultant. During that kick-off meeting their new leader will, among other things, answer their questions in an open forum. The consultant needs to emphasize that the objective of the process is to ensure a smooth and rapid integration of the new leader into the organization with a special emphasis on the new leader's team. Through introductory remarks by the consultant in each interview, the direct reports will understand both the benefits to their responding candidly and the consultant's role in the process. By reinforcing the goal of a smooth transition for the new leader, there is a greater likelihood that the information gathered in these interviews will be useful and that each of the direct reports will participate in the process with a positive attitude, up to, including and following the kick-off meeting on the first day. A sample list of questions to ask the direct reports includes the following:

How would you describe the culture of the organization (and your division/department)?

This question was asked of both the new leader's boss and peer group. It is important to hear the perspective of the new leader's direct reports as a basis of comparison. Look for similarities and discrepancies in their answers and ensure that this information is conveyed to the new leader.

What is currently working well in your department (division, etc.)?

The direct reports have strong opinions about what is working well and will be very interested in sustaining those things they believe are already working. Each individual gets to focus on the positive aspects of the organization. Respondents will typically answer this question thoughtfully because they naturally want to represent the organization, their department or division, and themselves in a positive light.

What are the short-term opportunities that could improve the organization's (or department's) performance?

This question is phrased more positively than simply asking, "What is not working well?" The aim is to get at the low hanging fruit that the new leader can address with them early in the transition, thus securing some early wins. There may be some reluctance at first to answer this question candidly, which the consultant will need to minimize. Once all of the direct reports have been interviewed, a trend line should emerge from this question. The answers will also either support or contradict the comments received in the boss and peer interviews. Knowing this information in advance will help the new leader move discussions in the right direction during the kick-off meeting with the direct reports on the first day and prioritize effectively during the first weeks on the job.

How do your customers (internal and external) view your organization?

People within any organization have perceptions (accurate or not) as to how their customers view them. A customer in this case applies not only to a paying customer, but also to internal organization customers. The marketing department's direct customers are the sales force that depends on them for direction and support: Are products announced in a timely manner and in a way that can help boost sales?

Are products branded well against the competition? The human resources department's customers are the employees as well as senior management: Are employees being developed properly? Are the benefit plans managed well? Is HR viewed by senior management as being a strategic asset in addition to being an administrative center for employees? The operations division's customers include the sales force, as well: Do they develop new products in a timely manner? Do the products work properly? The hospital laboratory's customers are every physician who sends a request for lab tests. Every department within an organization has its customers, and they all have opinions about the quality of service that is provided to them.

The answers to this question are very informative. The boss and peers will have been asked the same question pertaining to the new leader's area of responsibility. Once every direct report has responded, the consultant can piece together an accurate picture of the perceptions that exist with regard to the department or division that the new executive will soon lead.

From your perspective, what should the new leader focus on in the first 30, 60 and 90 days?

As with the question pertaining to customer perceptions, this one has also been asked of every participant in the process: boss (or board), peers and direct reports. Each direct report will have opinions regarding organizational priorities and what needs to be addressed first. If the direct reports vary in their responsibilities, the answers to this question may likewise vary, which is good for the new leader. More perspectives are better. The new leader will then know the high priorities that each member of the team holds and why. This information also has the potential of surfacing any potential problem areas. It may be that some of the direct reports want to see things done that are a direct contradiction to what the boss and peers want accomplished or advise doing.

By breaking this question down into 30-day increments, it also illuminates for the new leader what the team views as the higher priorities. A by-product of the New Leader Integration process is a prioritization of everything. Secure early wins, yes, but secure them in the right sequence if it is important to do so.

After collecting this information, the consultant should ask what each member sees as distant priorities as well. For example, what is lying out several months in the future that should be a critical win, and what will the short-term wins do (or fail to do if missed) in achieving intermediate and long-range goals? The detailed viewpoints of the direct reports will supplement the information previously shared by the new leader's boss and peers who likely have broader perspectives.

What would you like to see the new leader do differently from the previous leader?

As the saying goes, "Speak now or forever hold your peace." Every direct report will have experienced behaviors or ways of doing business in the previous leader that they would like to see come to an end. This is especially likely to be the case if the previous leader was unpopular and/or has been replaced due to inadequate performance. With that said, even outstanding previous leaders will have operated in certain ways that, for whatever reason, a direct report would like to see done differently. If what the direct report wants to see accomplished differently makes good business sense, then it is a good opportunity for the new leader to adjust. It will be noticed.

The consultant may experience some reluctance from direct reports to candidly respond to this question, especially if the previous leader is still within the organization. However, they must be reminded that these insights can go a long way toward improving their operation and environment. New leaders do take this information to heart and work to ensure that they do not create additional challenges by continuing unnecessary or counter-productive behaviors and practices.

What would you like to see the new leader do the same as the previous leader?

There are almost always behaviors and practices that worked well for a previous leader, even one being replaced for a lack of effectiveness. Those appropriate behaviors and practices need to be noted and sustained by the new leader if at all possible. Doing so will help mitigate the already disruptive nature of a leadership change, even in the best of circumstances.

In situations where the outgoing leader was highly regarded, the answers to this question will help the new leader know which behaviors and practices resulted in the direct reports' most positive responses. Changing those positive behaviors and practices of the previous leader may take the organization down the wrong road. The new leader can always adjust downstream, but if it is not necessary to do so early in the process, wait. Accentuate the positives in the early weeks and build on that. Change down the road will be better accepted if there is a solid foundation upon which to make those decisions.

What would you like to see the new leader do that the previous leader did not do?

This question should not be confused with what the new leader should do differently. Rather, it focuses on a wish list of sorts. Every member of the new leader's team will likely have something that he or she would like to have seen done in the previous administration. Often these are ideas that for one reason or another, the previous leader was reluctant to implement or did not see as a high priority. It could be that guidance given by the new leader's boss and peers supports this departmental wish list. Likewise, it could be that the guidance received by the boss and peers suggests just the opposite. As with every question, the objective is to help the new leader to know where to focus as well as what to avoid.

What should the new leader avoid doing at all costs?

Well thought out answers to this question could be a godsend to a new leader. Direct reports often have keen insights into what a new leader must avoid doing at all costs. We all can relate to this question.

How do you best respond to being led and managed?

Few change management consultants will have difficulty getting candid answers to this question. Everybody has a preferred way of being led and managed. You will hear such things as: "I'm good at what I do. I know my job. Just give me mission-oriented instructions and turn me loose. I'll keep the new boss informed on a regular basis and ask for assistance if I need it." Other individuals could have a less confident response such as, "I operate best when the boss just tells me what he/she wants done and then lets me do it."

There are many different answers to this question, but the trend line that results is either that the direct reports are very experienced and confident, mature in their field and need a minimum amount of guidance, to one where there is uncertainty and a lack of confidence. In some cases there will be a mixture of both. Regardless, the new leader will gain a great deal of insight about the direct reports through this question and if taken to heart, will lead and manage them accordingly until it is obvious that an adjustment needs to be made in the way individuals should be managed. It could be that the individual who wants to be left alone should be closely managed and that the person who needs a lot of direction could, with a modicum of coaching, be more confident, independent and productive via the support received from a new leader.

What are your key areas of responsibility and tasks?

In most cases this information will not have been readily available to a new leader. Soon after the start date, the new leader will be meeting one-on-one with every team member who participated in the process. The more information the new leader has in preparation for those initial meetings, the better they will go. If job descriptions exist, they should be collected by the consultant and provided to the new leader. Perhaps there is other documentation that illustrates responsibilities and tasks as well. If they do not exist, it would be helpful for direct reports to draft a short document that outlines their individual duties and responsibilities. The consultant can then provide this information to the new leader ahead of the start date.

What metrics have you been assigned?

Direct reports should be able to provide the metrics under which they operate. In addition to the metrics themselves, in whatever form they exist, there should be a current scorecard on those metrics available. If there is some other way for the new leader to obtain this information, that would be acceptable. The goal is for the new leader to get as much measurable data as possible in advance of the start date. If the consultant can discern how each direct report is doing against key performance indicators, the sooner the new leader can get a grasp on how well the group is performing. It also gives the new leader substantive information that direct reports will likely want to discuss in their initial one-on-one meeting with the new leader in the days immediately following the kick-off meeting. Any information of this nature collected by the consultant would be presented to the new leader along with the document that captured the responses to the interview questions of the direct reports and others. This gives the new leader time to review this information in advance of the start date.

In the absence of metrics or key performance indicators, the new leader will need to quickly establish a means of fact-based analysis. Knowing early in the assignment what is being measured and what is not is important information for the new leader to have going in.

What do you want the new leader to know about you?

This question can be disarming to a direct report. What does the new leader need to know? Answers can range from stressing a past record of high performance to currently being enrolled in a graduate school program. Sometimes this answer can disclose some very personal information. An employee could have a personal problem that the previous boss fully understood and worked around. It could be something such as having a disabled relative that needs weekly care that may necessitate the need for some flextime. The previous boss may have fully understood this and willingly accommodated the individual. An employee in a situation like this is going to be reticent to tell a new boss in the first week that such a need for special accommodation exists.

New bosses, when they hear about these things in advance of the start date, can build a lot of good will in the organization by approaching that individual privately the first day or two and acknowledging the situation and remedy. It may also be appropriate for the incoming leader to have the consultant carry the message back to the individual even prior to the start date. In the end, things get done better, sooner, if individuals are not angst-ridden over any issue that may cause a problem with their new boss. The consultant provides an especially valuable role in situations like this. The new leader will have been fully briefed on each individual's personal input before the kick-off meeting.

What do you want to know about the new leader?

This in many ways is the most important question asked of the direct reports. The consultant assures each individual that the question will not be attributed to him or her. All of these questions are anonymous. Why is that important? Simply this: The new leader's direct reports have the opportunity to ask the tough questions early on, the ones that are nagging or weighing on them. It takes the heat off the individual that these questions will be presented to the new leader anonymously. Few people want to risk getting off on the wrong foot with a new boss by asking a tough, direct question before a relationship has been established—especially, in a public forum. But how these questions get answered will speak volumes about the new leader. A past example of one such question was, "Have you ever managed a department consisting of all women before?" This one was posed to a new boss, a man, who was taking over a department of all women whose previous two bosses had been women. Another question, posed by a marketing professional, was aimed at determining if he had a future (or his colleagues for that matter) in the new leader's organization. The department's emphasis was on promotional material development and less on market research, prior to the leadership change. The new leader had been hired to take product promotions and advertising to a new level, with the proper justification to do so. In short, the person wanted to know if the new leader was going to have to replace any of them in order to achieve that balance.

So what is done with all of these anonymous questions? The consultant will collate them into the document that will be presented to the new leader for review. The goal, aside from the obvious one of knowing what the tough questions are going to be in advance, is that the new leader will use these questions to establish a proper tone in the kick-off meeting on the start date. Each anonymous question will be candidly answered by the new leader early in the kick-off meeting.

The Direct Reports' Sample Interview Questions

1. How would you describe the culture of the organization (and your division/department)?

2. What is currently working well in your department (division, etc.)?

3. What are the short-term opportunities that could improve the department's overall performance?

4. How do your customers (internal and external) view your organization?

5. From your perspective, what should the new leader focus on in the first 30, 60, 90 days?

6. What would you like for the new leader to do differently from the previous leader?

7. What would you like to see the new leader do the same as the previous leader?

8. What would you like to see the new leader do that the previous leader did not do?

9. What should the new leader avoid doing at all cost?

10. How do you best respond to being led and managed?

11. What are your key areas of responsibility and tasks?

12. What metrics have you been assigned?

13. What do you want the new leader to know about you?

14. What do you want to know about the new leader?

CHAPTER 8

Other Possible Interviews

I t may be appropriate on occasion to interview other stake-holders. They vary from organization to organization and the questions asked need to be specific for that stakeholder. Interviews in the for-profit sector may include key custom-ers, e.g., those who serve as your beta test site managers, or the biggest customers, or those who have been with you the longest, or the ones who have had the most issues and yet are still with you, etc. Key supplier executives or repre-sentatives might also be interviewed. In the nonprofit sector, likely interviews may include key donors or some selected members of the board of trustees—even if the new leader is not in the top position. In healthcare organizations, if a new hospital executive is arriving, it may be appropriate to interview some prominent medical practice group administrators or key admitting physicians. Universities might want to involve selected members of the board of trustees or their alumni association.

There are many situations where input from others, in addition to the boss, peers and direct reports would be valued by the new leader. These individuals need to be identified by the hiring manager before the consultant launches the project. Internal administrative staff members should be involved in coordinating those interviews.

CHAPTER 9

The Kick-off Meeting

While the boss is more interested in results, and the peers are more interested in how the new leader's presence will impact their own functional areas, the direct reports are the ones who feel the pressure of a new leader. Like it or not, things are about to change. The new leader's team can only hope those changes are for the better. This phase of the New Leader Integration process—the kick-off meeting—will have a substantial impact on how the new leader and direct reports communicate and work together. The meeting is as important for the new leader as it is for the direct reports. New leaders work hard to succeed. Good leaders prefer to succeed in a collaborative, trusting, team environment. Direct reports want to know they can trust and depend upon their new leader.

The kick-off meeting occurs on the new leader's start date. It will be held in the morning or the afternoon, depending upon what other appointments the new leader will have that day. The meeting will last for approximately three hours (with a break in the middle). It is best for this meeting to occur off site, but regardless, a private setting is necessary with no interruptions.

Refreshments should be provided that are appropriate for the time of day. This is an important, though informal meeting, so setting the right tone is important.

The consultant will begin the meeting by reviewing the New Leader Integration process events to date. Following these remarks the consultant will outline the agenda. There are basically five parts to the meeting:

- Introduction of the new leader

- The new leader's opening comments

- The new leader's addressing of the anonymous questions

- Break

- Open discussion with the new leader on topics of his or her choosing

The consultant will introduce the new leader with as much information as is appropriate for that meeting's setting.

The first 15 minutes or so the new leader delivers some opening remarks. They should set the tone for the remainder of the meeting and begin to build the collegiality that will be important going forward. The essential leader traits that must be conveyed are transparency and authenticity. Trust and open communication must begin to develop as rapidly as possible.

Following the new leader's opening remarks, he or she will answer all of the anonymous questions that were gathered during the interviews. How each question is sequenced and presented depends upon the comfort level of the new leader.

Answering these questions will take approximately one hour. The group would then take a 20-minute break for refreshments.

Following the break, the new leader will set the stage for the remainder of the meeting. During the debriefing a few days earlier, the consultant and new leader will have isolated several discussion topics that were derived from all of the interviews. The objective for this part of the meeting is to get the group interacting around topics of immediate importance to the new leader. Provided the first half of the meeting went well, the group discussion should progress freely and openly. This last phase of the meeting should go for approximately one hour, but it should not be rushed. The topics identified for discussion need to be substantive ones with which the direct reports will readily identify. This is an excellent opportunity for the new leader to observe how the group interacts and communicates with him or her.

Once these discussions end, the new leader should close the meeting on a high note and remind the attendees that one-on-one meetings with each of them will be scheduled quickly (preferably within a week at the most). Any general topics the new leader will want to discuss during each of these individual meetings should be identified at this time.

A suggested agenda is at <u>Appendix D</u>.

CHAPTER 10

Time Considerations

The most significant challenges to successfully implementing a New Leader Integration process are the time
commitment and constraints on the part of the consultant coupled with the number of people to be interviewed
and their availability.

In most cases the consultant will conduct the interviews
on-site. Occasionally it may be necessary for the consultant to travel to multiple locations. Whenever possible these
interviews should be accomplished face-to-face.

In every case the organization will need to appoint a
coordinator for these interviews. Often the executive assistant of the person initiating the project accomplishes this.
The consultant will need to stay in close communication
with this individual to ensure that every meeting takes place

at the appropriate time and place. Last minute cancellations will need to be rescheduled promptly.

Normally the consultant will block out two to three days on-site to conduct these interviews. More time will be necessary if travel to multiple locations is involved.

Once the interviews are completed, the consultant will compile all information gathered into a well organized, informative and easy to read document to be given to the new leader. If the consultant is not interrupted, this can take two days to complete. A suggested format for this report is found at Appendix C.

The document is then provided to the new leader who will be given two to three days to review it, followed by a one-on-one meeting with the consultant that will take most of a day to complete. The consultant will be a rich source of information and insights and the new leader will see the value of the information that has been captured in the process. The document will prompt a myriad of questions that need to be answered to the satisfaction of the new leader. Some of the questions may lack obvious answers. In that case the consultant must strive to track down the answers to those questions and get back to the new leader as soon as possible.

Assuming everything goes according to plan and the interview sessions are well coordinated, the consultant can expect to devote from eight to ten days from start to finish for a thorough New Leader Integration project. A day or two more may be necessary if there is additional travel involved. A typical project schedule looks this way:

Interviews:	2-3 days
Writing:	1-2 days
Debriefing:	1 day
Kick-off Meeting:	1 day
30-day Follow-Up	1 day
60-day Follow-Up	1 day
90-day Follow-Up	1 day

One way to ensure that this compressed time schedule does not impact the quality of the project is to begin the interviews as the hiring decision is coming to a close and an offer is being negotiated to conclusion. This will save time and the responses and guidance of those being interviewed will be current. The document can even be drafted during that time. In short, consultants will need to gauge the workload anticipated against the timeframe for the hiring process to reach closure and the new leader's start date.

Another consideration is that the consultant will need to meet the likely new leader ahead of time. This is essential and is best accomplished during the interviews of the finalists. This will allow the consultant to prepare the new leader mentally for the process, answer any questions, and address any concerns that may arise. It is important to ensure that this process is not sprung upon the new leader at the last minute by the organization or by a consultant who is a perfect stranger.

It is likely that New Leader Integration projects will be conducted for a high number of internal managers who are moving up or over to new responsibilities. The process is the same except for timing and will usually happen quickly once a reassignment decision is made or a promotion takes place. The human resources executive may need to slow the transition enough to allow for the New Leader Integration process to be accomplished. If an appropriate internal consultant is not available, contact the pool of available external consultants to identify someone who is available to conduct this process. Ideally, with proper coordination, this would have happened before the promotion announcement.

The three follow-up meetings with the new leader and the boss that will occur at 30-day intervals should be scheduled. In advance of these meetings, the consultant and the new leader will need to discuss how well the integration is proceeding, where key tasks are behind schedule, what actions are being taken to get back on schedule, and identify any additional guidance that may be needed from the boss in order for the new leader to accomplish his or her integration objectives. The purpose for these follow-up meetings is for the new leader and the boss to touch base regularly regarding the actions that were identified as most important during the first 90 days. The consultant is present for each of those meetings to ensure that the essential points are adequately addressed and documented.

PART III

NEW LEADER INTEGRATION PROCESS ENHANCERS

CHAPTER 11

Tools to Aid in New Leader Integration

I f there are organization development professionals on staff, there is a likelihood that they use various tools and assessments to improve managerial and team effectiveness. These tools can range from the Myers-Briggs Type Indicator (MBTI) to the Personal Profiling System that is based on the "DISC" model, as well as many others. If your organization has incorporated the use of these tools, more often than not your managers will have already been profiled. Increasingly, the executives you recruit from the outside may also have knowledge of and personal experience with these types of instruments. These tools can be very useful for the integration of new leaders. A thoroughly developed executive transition program should integrate a variety of profiling tools like these into the process wherever possible.

Due to its ease of use, the DISC profile can be particularly helpful. DISC is an acronym for *Dominant, Influence, Steady* and *Conscientious*. The profile determines an individual's temperament and behavioral style and shows how each style can be a help or a hindrance to an individual depending on the situation.

This awareness can make a difference when integrating a new leader. For example, the more the direct reports know in advance about the behavioral style of their new boss, the more they will be able to adapt to that temperament, especially if the new leader's and previous leader's styles are significantly different.

If your organization is serious about implementing and sustaining a New Leader Integration program throughout your organization, you will find that implementing a personal profiling tool such as DISC at the same time may enhance the effectiveness of your executive integration process.

CHAPTER 12

Executive Coaching

Executive coaching has proved to be the most effective developmental vehicle for executives. An experienced executive coach can serve a larger role than a leadership or management developer. A good executive coach can also serve as a sounding board and guide during leader transitions. The one-on-one private nature of the coaching process works especially well in this role.

One reason why a coach can be so effective in executive transitions is that new leaders are not likely to have developed collegial or mentor relationships with peers or a boss. There are few, if any, people they can turn to for candid advice as to how best to navigate the waters of their new organizations. If executive coaching is determined to be an addition to a New Leader Integration program, all transitioning leaders should be assigned a coach. If every new leader is assigned a coach, most new leaders will welcome the resource.

In the hustle and bustle of assuming a new position, new leaders often feel the pressure to make quick decisions just to keep things moving. The blueprint for success provided by the New Leader Integration process helps them stay on course. An executive coach who is aware of the contents of that blueprint can assist a new leader in following it.

Assuming that the studies cited earlier regarding the attrition rates of executives are accurate, it stands to reason that everything should be done to ensure the success of new leaders. Too much is at stake to leave the success of the new leader to hope or chance. The addition of an executive coach at the end of a New Leader Integration process can help ensure that the new leader continues to advance in the right direction once onboard.

In some cases, the likely choice for this executive coaching role will be the consultant who oversaw the New Leader Integration process and who would merely assume a follow-on assignment. There are advantages and disadvantages to this approach. While the fresh eyes of a newly assigned coach can be an advantage to a new leader, there may have developed such a degree of trust between a new leader and process consultant that continuing the relationship could be the best method. Each situation is unique.

AFTERWORD

There are numerous bottom line business reasons to compress the time it takes for new leaders to reach their full potential. If there were no tangible benefits to integrating new leaders effectively, you likely would not have read this book. Yet there are other reasons to provide a New Leader Integration process for incoming executives, though they will not likely drive an organization's decision to do so.

Consider again that each year approximately half a million managers will take on new roles in the Fortune 500 alone. This statistic does not take into account nonprofit organizations, healthcare systems and hospitals, colleges and universities, government agencies, etc. As we have learned, the experts tell us that anywhere from 30 to 50 percent of these new leaders will not succeed, many of whom will already be gone by the end of the second year. This is a staggering casualty rate. In some cases the unsuccessful managers will be kept on the payroll and either demoted or moved laterally to another position in which they may have a higher likelihood of success. But the irrefutable truth is that many—tens of thousands if the statistics are correct—are no longer on the payroll and have either moved on to another job or are more likely looking for one.

It is not only a company's bottom line that is impacted by such preventable turnover, but also the impact of failure on these leaders' personal lives that is at stake.

It is easy for the habitually successful executive to dismiss the failures of others. We should keep in mind, however, that almost every new leader who was hired or promoted was previously successful prior to failing in a new job. In the case of outside hires, the new leaders recruited were most likely at the top of the candidate pyramid. Internal promotions most often are based on the observations of the organizations' top leaders as to how well those individuals performed in other roles.

There is a high likelihood that if you are reading this, you have seen at least one promising colleague separated from your organization for failure to perform to the level needed and expected. We do not like to dwell on these situations.

When new leaders are hired from the outside or promoted from within, there are often family relocations involved. Accepting a new position involves taking a risk. Few people who take on new leadership roles are aware of the high attrition rate associated with these moves. If they were, they might think twice about accepting that new job.

The point here is that there are other costs associated with executive failures in addition to the bottom line. There are personal costs, such as the impact on the failed executive's family. When a new leader's family relocates or a successful manager leaves a secure job for the allure of advancement and the change does not work out, many people's lives are disrupted. Were these job losses preventable?

As the saying goes, "An ounce of prevention is worth a pound of cures." It is time for organizations to be proactive in ensuring that their new leaders succeed. More needs to be done than simply improving the selection process. While it is true many leader failures are due to ineffective hiring practices, the studies do not support that poor hiring decisions are at the root of the high attrition problem. There are measures that can be taken to effectively integrate new leaders and thereby increase their likelihood of succeeding in both the short and long-term. The process outlined in this book is but one way to do this. Think about that the next time you see an otherwise promising new executive fail to succeed in your organization.

Appendix A: New Leader Integration Process Sequence

Step 1:   Select process consultant(s) (internal, external or recruiter).

Step 2:   Agree upon a New Leader Integration process template and brief the consultant(s).

Step 3:   Consultant meets candidate finalists in the interview cycle (briefs the process).

Step 4:   Candidate is hired (or promoted).

Step 5:   Consultant is alerted of the hire or promotion and is engaged.

Step 6:   Interviews are scheduled with all stakeholders.

Step 7:   Consultant speaks with new leader to identify questions he or she will want answered.

Step 8:   Consultant conducts interviews (boss or board, peers, direct reports, others).

Step 9:   "Blueprint for Success" document is prepared by consultant.

Step 10:   New leader is provided the document for review.

Step 11:   New leader and consultant meet for detailed discussion of the Blueprint for Success.

Step 12:   New leader and consultant prepare for the kick-off meeting on the start date.

Step 13:   Kick-off meeting is scheduled and attendees are notified.

Step 14:   Consultant facilitates the kick-off meeting with the new leader and the direct reports.

Step 15:   Consultant and new leader de-brief following the kick off meeting and plan next steps.

Step 16:   Consultant follows up with the new leader and boss at 30, 60 and 90 day intervals.

Appendix B: New Leader Integration Sample Questions

The Boss (or Board) Interview Questions

General Questions

1. How would you describe the culture of the organization?
2. What type of executive fits in well at this organization?
3. What type of executive does NOT fit in well at this organization?
4. What problems or hurdles has the organization faced in the past two years?
5. What problems or hurdles has the new leader's department faced in the past two years?
6. What are your most important values?
7. What sets this organization apart from the competition?
8. What rumors, good or bad, exist in the marketplace pertaining to your organization?
9. How would you describe your management team?
10. What worked well for the predecessor in the job (and not so well)?

11. What was the background of the last person in the position?

12. What was lacking in the background/skill set of the last person in the position?

13. How do you see the current business situation (Turn-around? Sustainment? Other?)

Specific Questions

14. How do you want the new leader to communicate with you (What medium?)?

15. How frequently do you want the new leader to communicate with you (and in what level of detail)?

16. What types of issues and decisions require consultation with you in advance?

17. How will the new leader's performance be measured?

18. What factors (soft and hard) make the new leader's business situation a challenge?

19. What are the key challenges that the new leader will face in the first 90 days?

20. What specific projects need attention in the first 30, 60 and 90 days?

21. What will constitute the "must happens" in the first 90 days?

22. How do you view the new leader's team of people?

23. What should the new leader avoid (specific, known or potential pitfalls)?

24. What key resources are available to the new leader, or soon will be available or unavailable, or will remain unavailable?

25. What do you want to see done in the same way as the new leader's predecessor?

26. What do you want to see done differently than the new leader's predecessor?

The Peer Group's Interview Questions

1. How would you describe the culture of the organization?

2. What type of executive fits in at this organization?

3. What type of executive does NOT fit in at this organization?

4. From your perspective, what should the new leader focus on in the first 30, 60 and 90 days?

5. What does the new leader need to do to ensure your own continued effectiveness?

6. What does the new leader need to avoid doing to ensure your own effectiveness?

7. What do you want the new leader to continue to do that the predecessor did?

8. What do you want the new leader to stop doing that the predecessor did?

9. What do you want the new leader to start doing that the predecessor did not do?

10. From your perspective, how best is it to communicate with the boss (e.g., style, techniques)?

11. How do you want the new leader to communicate with you?

12. How do you generally and specifically view the new leader's staff?

13. What should the new leader avoid doing at all costs?

The Direct Reports' Interview Questions

1. How would you describe the culture of the organization (and your division/department)?

2. What is currently working well in your department (division, etc.)?

3. What are the short-term opportunities that could improve the department's overall performance?

4. How do your customers (internal and external) view your organization?

5. From your perspective, what should the new leader focus on in the first 30, 60, 90 days?

6. What would you like for the new leader to do differently from the previous leader?

7. What would you like to see the new leader do the same as the previous leader?

8. What would you like to see the new leader do that the previous leader did not do?

9. What should the new leader avoid doing at all cost?

10. How do you best respond to being led and managed?

11. What are your key areas of responsibility and tasks?

12. What metrics have you been assigned?

13. What do you want the new leader to know about you?

14. What do you want to know about the new leader?

Appendix C: New Leader Integration Document Outline

Section 1: General Questions Posed to the Boss (or Board) and Responses

—List each question and response (by name if there is more than one).

Section 2: Specific Questions Posed to the Boss (or Board) and Responses

—List each question and response (by name if there is more than one).

Section 3: Questions Posed to the Peer Group and Their Responses

—List each question and all responses, by name.

Section 4: Open Questions Posed to Direct Reports and Responses

—List each question and all responses, by name, under each question.

Section 5: Anonymous Questions Asked by the Direct Reports

—Just list the questions.

Section 6: What the Direct Reports Want the New Leader to Know About Them

–List each direct report's response by name.

Section 7: Potential Opportunities Arising During the Integration Process

–This is a summary based on the consultant's observations.

Section 8: Potential Conflicts Arising During the Integration Process

–This is a summary based on the consultant's observations.

Section 9: Points for Consideration in Preparation for the Kick-off Meeting

–This is specific guidance that has derived from all interviews.

Appendix D: New Leader Integration Kick-off Meeting Agenda

Suggested time allocation for the meeting is 3 ½ hours.

Hold the meeting off-site if possible (large conference table works well).

Have refreshments on-hand when everyone arrives.

<u>AGENDA</u>

Consultant welcomes participants	5 minutes
Consultant Introduces New Leader	5 minutes
New Leader's opening remarks	20 minutes
New Leader answers anonymous questions	60 minutes
Break with refreshments	20 minutes
New Leader's discussion topics with direct reports	60 minutes
Closing remarks	10 minutes

NOTE: It is important that the new leader schedule a face-to-face meeting with ALL participants in this process (boss, peers, direct reports and others). The meetings should occur by the end of the first week or as soon as possible. The Blueprint for Success will provide meaningful information and discussion topics for those meetings.

Made in the USA
Lexington, KY
05 August 2013